UTRECHT
TRAVEL GUIDE
2024

"Immerse Yourself in Utrecht, Netherlands Nature's Beauty and Adventures"

Gary D. Kinman

Table of Contents

1. INTRODUCTION

Utrecht, a beguiling city settled in the core of the Netherlands, enthralls guests with its rich history, beautiful waterways, and dynamic social embroidery. In this far-reaching guide, we will dive into the quintessence of Utrecht, giving a savvy outline and a brief look into its celebrated past.

Outline of Utrecht

Utrecht's Geographic Magnificence

Arranged in the focal piece of the Netherlands, Utrecht flaunts an ideal place along the banks of the Waterway Rhine.

The city's geology is described by an organization of winding channels that confuse through its noteworthy focus, making a beautiful and serene mood. Utrecht is frequently hailed for its all-around saved middle-age design, upgrading the charm of its roads and streams.

Social Mixture

Utrecht remains a lively social center point, drawing in specialists, understudies, and history lovers the same. The city is home to a different populace, adding to an exuberant air and a combination of different practices. As one investigates its roads, the mix of advancement and custom becomes obvious in the diverse cluster of shops, bistros, and social foundations.

Instructive Nexus

Eminent for its regarded college, established in 1636, Utrecht has for quite some time been a middle for scholastic greatness. The college upgrades the city's scholarly dynamic quality as well as adds to its energetic energy, because of a huge understudy populace. This scholastic legacy has made a permanent imprint on Utrecht's character, cultivating a climate of learning and development.

Green Desert Springs in the Metropolitan Wilderness

Utrecht shocks guests with its obligation to green spaces amid the metropolitan turn of events. Stops and gardens speck the cityscape, offering peaceful retreats for the two local people and vacationers. Griftpark, with its extensive yards and lakes, and the memorable greenhouses are only several instances of Utrecht's obligation to safeguard nature inside the metropolitan climate.

Brief History

Old Roots

Utrecht's set of experiences can be traced back to Roman times when it filled in as an urgent stronghold along the northern lines of the Roman Domain. Throughout the long term, the city developed into a strict focus, acquiring conspicuousness with the foundation of St. Martin's House of God in the seventh 100 years.

Religious Force to be reckoned with

During the Medieval times, Utrecht turned into a critical ministerial focus, with the House of Prayer filling in as the seat of the Archbishopric of Utrecht. The city's strict impact stretched out past its boundaries, assuming an essential part in the more extensive European setting.

The Dom Pinnacle: A Demonstration of Utrecht's Inheritance

At the core of Utrecht stands the notable Dom Pinnacle, an image of the city's strength and perseverance through the ages. Development of the House of God and its pinnacle started in the fourteenth hundred years, and albeit the nave of the church building fell in a tempest in 1674, the Dom Pinnacle remains a superb sign of Utrecht's middle-age magnificence.

Brilliant Age Flourishing

Utrecht thrived during the Dutch Brilliant Age, encountering financial flourishing and social development. The city's channels, fixed with dealer houses, tell stories of this well-to-do period. Utrecht's essential area along shipping lanes added to its business achievement, making a permanent imprint on its building and monetary scene.

Present-day Renaissance

In later times, Utrecht has gone through a cutting-edge renaissance, embracing development while safeguarding its verifiable appeal. The city's obligation to the practical metropolitan turn of events and social variety has situated it as a model for contemporary European urban communities.

Conclusion

All in all, Utrecht's appeal lies not just in its beautiful trenches and memorable tourist spots but also in the unique transaction between its rich history and forward-looking soul. As we explore the different features of this dazzling city, we welcome you to drench yourself in the pith of Utrecht, where the past consistently converges with the present.

2. GETTING TO UTRECHT

Welcome to Utrecht, an enchanting city in the core of the Netherlands! Exploring your direction here is a breeze, and I'm here to direct you through the intricate details of getting to Utrecht.

Transportation Options

Utrecht is very much associated, offering different transportation choices to suit each explorer's inclinations. The Dutch are known for their affection for cycling, and Utrecht is no exception. Get a bicycle, and you'll feel nearby as you pedal through the pleasant roads. If cycling isn't your thing, dread not — Utrecht flaunts an effective public transportation framework, including transports and cable cars.

For the people who lean toward a more loosened-up venture, consider cruising along the trenches that breeze through the city. Utrecht's streams give a special point of view and a comfortable option in contrast to customary transportation. Whether by bicycle, transport, cable car, or boat, you're certain to track down a method of transport that accommodates your style.

Worldwide and Nearby Airports

Landing in Utrecht is a breeze because its vicinity is very much associated with worldwide and neighborhood air terminals. Amsterdam Air Terminal Schiphol, one of Europe's significant center points, is around 45 minutes away via train. From Schiphol, successive direct trains will whisk you to Utrecht Focal Station, the city's transportation center point.

On the off chance that you lean toward a more straightforward appearance, Eindhoven Air terminal is another choice. While more modest, it offers a helpful entryway to Utrecht, situated about an hour away via train or vehicle. Remember that the Netherlands' productive train network guarantees smooth progress from the air terminal to the core of Utrecht.

Utrecht itself is served by a neighborhood air terminal, Rotterdam The Hague Air terminal, giving extra choices to those flying locally or from neighboring European objections. In any case, most worldwide explorers view Schiphol as the essential door to Utrecht.

Public Transportation inside the City

Whenever you show up in Utrecht, exploring the city is an enjoyment with its efficient public transportation framework. The broad transport organization and productive cable car administrations make it simple to investigate everywhere. Utrecht Focal Station fills in as the fundamental transportation center, associating you consistently with various pieces of the city and then some.

Five fundamental focuses to remember while using public transportation in Utrecht:

1. U-OV Chipkaart: To board transports and cable cars, you'll require a U-OV Chipkaart, a battery-powered savvy card. Buy one at Utrecht Focal Station or different deals focused all through the city. It guarantees a smooth excursion without the problem of purchasing tickets each time.

2. Central Area of the Station: Utrecht Focal Station is decisively situated in the downtown area, making it an ideal

beginning stage for your investigations. Exploit the very much-stamped exits and passageways to find your direction to various pieces of Utrecht without any problem.

3. Frequent and Dependable Services: Utrecht's public transportation is known for its unwavering quality. Transports and cable cars run as often as possible, sticking to a tight timetable. Plan your excursions with certainty, realizing that you won't sit tight for a long time.

4. Biking Society Integration: Utrecht is a bicycle-accommodating city, and this stretches out to its public transportation. Many transports and cable cars are

outfitted with bicycle racks, permitting you to flawlessly consolidate cycling with different methods of transport.

5. Scenic Trench Routes: For a one-of-a-kind encounter, consider taking a water transport along Utrecht's charming channels. It's not only a method of transportation; a grand excursion gives an alternate point of view of the city's excellence.

Conclusion

All in all, getting to Utrecht is a cheerful excursion loaded with choices taking care of different inclinations. Here, the city's productive public transportation guarantees that investigating the beguiling roads, trenches, and social fortunes is a consistent and superb experience. In this way, jump on a bicycle, get a cable car, or coast along the trenches — the charming city of Utrecht anticipates your revelation!

3. ACCOMMODATION

Welcome to the superb city of Utrecht, where finding the ideal convenience improves your general insight. We should jump into the range of choices accessible to suit each explorer's requirements.

Hotels and Housing Choices

1. Luxury Retreats: Utrecht brags a determined first-rate inn offering a mix of tastefulness and solace. The notorious Fantastic Inn Karel V, set in a previous cloister, remains a demonstration of extravagance. With roomy rooms, top-notch food, and a spa, it's a shelter for those looking for lavishness.

2. Boutique Charm: For a more cozy stay, consider store inns like Mary K Inn. Settled in the core of the city, these foundations frequently highlight one-of-a-kind style, customized administration, and comfortable air, giving a brilliant usual hangout spot.

3. Modern Comfort: If smooth and contemporary is your inclination, Utrecht has a scope of current lodgings. The NH Community Utrecht, with its moderate plan and focal area, takes special care of the individuals who value a bit of metropolitan refinement.

4. Family- Accommodating Accommodations: Going with little ones?

Family-accommodating inns like Mother Goose Lodging offer a warm greeting and conveniences taking care of the requirements of the two guardians and kids, guaranteeing a significant stay for the entire family.

5. Historical Stays: Drench yourself in the city's rich history by picking convenience in a notable structure. The Eye Lodging, set in a previous eye emergency clinic, joins verifiable fascination with current solace, giving an exceptional and essential experience.

Regions to Remain in Utrecht

1. City Center: The core of Utrecht, the downtown area, is ideally suited for the

people who need to be amidst everything. You'll track down noteworthy tourist spots, clamoring markets, and an energetic nightlife. Inns like the NH Community Utrecht offer simple admittance to the city's fundamental attractions.

2. Grachten District: For a beautiful stay, consider the Grachten Region, with its beguiling waterways and notable design. This region offers a more loosened-up air while as yet being near Utrecht's social areas of interest.

3. Lombok: Searching for multicultural energy? Lombok, known for its different local areas and worldwide food, gives an extraordinary encounter. Financial plan

cordial facilities like the Court Inn are reachable, making it a fantastic decision for explorers on a careful spending plan.

4. Eastern District: If you lean toward a calmer climate, the Eastern Region may be the best decision. With its green spaces and private feel, this region offers a quiet retreat. Consider remaining at the Malie Inn, which mixes serenity with openness to the downtown area.

5. University Quarter: Drench yourself in the scholastic air by remaining close to the college. The region is exuberant with understudy exercises and offers a scope of reasonable facilities, pursuing a spending plan cordial decision for explorers.

Spending Plan Well Disposed of Facilities

1. Hostels: Utrecht gives a variety of inns taking special care of economical voyagers. The Stayokay Utrecht Centrum, situated close to Neude Square, offers reasonable dorm-style rooms, making it a superb decision for explorers.

2. Guesthouses: Picking a guesthouse can give a comfortable and savvy elective. Anna's Bed and Breakfast, with its customized administration and simple air, offers a wonderful stay without burning through every last dollar.

3. Short-Term Rentals: Investigate the city like a neighborhood by picking

momentary rentals. Stages like Airbnb include an assortment of spending plan well-disposed choices, from private rooms to whole lofts, permitting you to fit your convenience to your requirements.

4. Budget Hotels: A few financial plan lodgings in Utrecht, like Inn Ibis Utrecht, offer reasonable rates without settling on fundamental conveniences. These foundations give an agreeable base for investigating the city without stressing your spending plan.

5. Student Accommodations: During the Christmas season, understudy facilities might open up for explorers. Consider checking college lodging choices for

reasonable and essential stays, particularly assuming you're OK with less difficult conveniences.

4. EXPLORING UTRECHT

Welcome to Utrecht, a city that easily mixes history with current appeal. As your educated local escort, we should set out on an excursion to investigate the enthralling features of Utrecht, disclosing its top attractions, unexpected, yet invaluable treasures, and rich social and verifiable destinations.

Top Attractions

I. Dom Pinnacle

Our experience starts with the notable Dom Pinnacle, gladly remaining the tallest church tower in the Netherlands. As we rise to its 465 stages, wonder about the all-encompassing perspectives on Utrecht's red-bricked roofs and rich plant life. The pinnacle, part of the Dom House of Prayer, describes hundreds of years of history, and you'll feel a significant association with the past as you arrive at the top.

II. Utrecht Trenches

Plan to be charmed as we wander along Utrecht's pleasant channels, suggestive of a postcard scene. Dissimilar to Amsterdam, Utrecht's trenches ooze a calmer appeal, fixed with dynamic bistros and memorable wharf basements. Embrace the neighborhood pace by taking a comfortable boat ride or walking around the Oudegracht, where exceptionally old structures tell stories of exchange and trade.

III. Rietveld Schröder House

A pearl of current engineering, the Rietveld Schröder House entices those with an appreciation for cutting-edge plans. Planned by Gerrit Rietveld in 1924, this UNESCO-recorded magnum opus is a living demonstration of the De Stijl development. Directed visits offer a brief look into the clever utilization of room and variety, making it a must-visit for craftsmanship and design devotees.

Unlikely Treasures

Utrecht, past its notable attractions, harbors brilliant unlikely treasures ready to be found.

Historical center Speelklok

Get a kick out of the capricious universe of self-playing instruments at Exhibition Hall Speelklok. From extremely old music boxes to robotized orchestras, this unexpected, yet invaluable treasure gives an entrancing excursion through the development of melodic craftsmanship.

Pandhof Sinte Marie

Get away from the metropolitan hustle and step into the quiet Pandhof Sinte

Marie, a secret patio garden near the Dom House of Prayer. Appreciate the middle-age engineering, fragrant blossoms, and serene climate — a desert garden concealed from the city's buzz.

De Haar Castle

Adventure right outside Utrecht to find the charming De Haar Palace. With its fantasy-like turrets and lavish nurseries, this palace offers a brief look into blue-blooded life. Investigate the lavish insides, walk around the finished grounds, and transport yourself to a pastime.

Social and Verifiable Locales

Utrecht's rich social embroidery is woven with verifiable milestones that reverberate stories of the past.

Centraal Museum

Plunge into Utrecht's creative legacy at the Centraal Gallery, lodging a noteworthy assortment going from middle-age strict workmanship to contemporary works. Try not to miss the Rietveld assortment, exhibiting the advancement of the Dutch plan.

St. Martin's Cathedral

Step back in time to St. Martin's House of God, a glorious Gothic design with attachments following back to the seventh hundred years. The church building's nave, transept, and sanctuaries hold hundreds of years of history, making it a convincing site for those fascinated by Utrecht's strict and designed past.

Utrecht College Museum

For a mix of schooling and diversion, visit the Utrecht College Historical Center. Uncover the logical tradition of Utrecht's college through shows going from interesting minerals to verifiable logical instruments, giving a remarkable viewpoint on the city's scholastic ability.

Conclusion

All in all, Utrecht entices travelers with its assorted contributions — from the archaic appeal of the Dom Pinnacle to the contemporary charm of the Rietveld Schröder House. As your aide, I trust this excursion through Utrecht has started your interest and left you with a more profound appreciation for this charming city. Blissful investigating!

5. DINING AND CUISINE

Eating and Food: A Sample of the Netherlands

Welcome, individual food fans, to the core of Dutch gastronomy. In this excursion, we'll investigate the flavors that make up the magnificent Dutch feasting scene, from nearby fortunes to famous diners and the vivacious road food culture.

I. Neighborhood Dutch Food: Divulging Culinary Delights

1. Stroopwafels - Sweet Ponders of Holland

Start your culinary experience with stroopwafels, meager waffle treats loaded with gooey caramel syrup. Found in each corner, these sweet treats are Dutch 1. Match them with a steaming mug of espresso for a real neighborhood experience.

2. Haring - A Strong Marine Adventure

Daring people, celebrate! Plunge into the universe of haring - crude fish presented with onions and pickles. It's an intense, customary dish that catches the pith of Dutch shoreline living. A consideration wandering into culinary investigation anticipates those ready to take a sample of the ocean.

3. Erwtensoep - Solace in a Bowl

At the point when the weather conditions turn crisp, embrace the glow of erwtensoep, a generous split pea soup. Loaded with peas, pork, and vegetables, this dish is a consoling embrace for your taste buds. Try not to botch the opportunity to relish this Dutch winter example.

4. Dutch Cheeses - A Dairy Darling's Dream

Cheddar fans, cheer! Gouda, Edam, Leyden - the rundown goes on. Dutch cheeses are a range of flavors ready to be investigated. Visit nearby business sectors and cheddar shops to test these pleasures, matching them with new Dutch apples for a basic yet fulfilling nibble.

5. Poffertjes - Little Flapjacks, Huge Delight

End your neighborhood culinary excursion with poffertjes, little soft hotcakes tidied with powdered sugar. Served hot and new, these superb nibbles are a sweet end to your investigation of Dutch food.

II. Famous Eateries and Bistros: Culinary Gems

1. De Kas (Amsterdam) - Where Nature Meets Cuisine

Settled in Amsterdam, De Kas offers a novel eating experience inside a nursery. Appreciate ranch-to-table dishes that develop with the seasons, guaranteeing an explosion of new and lively flavors in each nibble.

2. FG Food Labs (Rotterdam) - A Culinary Laboratory

Rotterdam's FG Food Labs is a shelter for those looking for vanguard eating. Gourmet specialist François Geurds makes inventive dishes that play with your faculties, consolidating culinary mastery with a bit of energy.

3. Café De Jaren (Amsterdam) - Waterside Bliss

For a loose bistro experience, go to Bistro De Jaren in Amsterdam. Sit by the waterway, tasting your beverage, and take in the laid-back environment. It's an ideal spot for a comfortable early lunch or a night wind-down.

4. Bazar (Rotterdam) - Fascinating Flavors in a Lively Setting

Drench yourself in the vivacious climate of Bazar in Rotterdam. This café offers a combination of Center Eastern and North African food, served in a dynamic, varied setting. Plan for a tangible excursion through different flavors.

5. Winkel 43 (Amsterdam) - Fruity dessert Extravaganza

Enjoy your sweet tooth at Winkel 43, popular for its tasty Dutch fruity dessert. Presented with a liberal spot of whipped cream, this notorious treat is a must-pursue for anybody with an affection for everything sweet.

III. Road Food and Markets: The Beat of Dutch Flavors

1. Bitterballen - Reduced down Bar Pleasure

Explore the roads and bars to find bitterballen, rotisserie spheres loaded up with an exquisite ragout. These brilliant pleasures are a staple in Dutch bars, giving the ideal ally to drinks all around.

2. Stroopwafel Stands - Sweet Road Treats

Investigate the roads for stroopwafel stands, where sellers make these sweet wonders just before your eyes. The smell of caramel drifts through the air as you witness the production of these luscious pleasures.

3. Patat - Dutch Fries Extravaganza

Patat, or Dutch fries, is a notable road food. Presented with a variety of fixings like mayo, ketchup, or even nut sauce, they're a firm enjoyment that fulfills any tidbit hankering.

4. Oliebollen - Dutch Donut Delights

During bubbly seasons, search out oliebollen stands. These broiled doughnuts, frequently sprinkled with powdered sugar, are a Dutch practice during New Year's festivals. Snatch a pack and participate in the celebrations.

5. Albert Cuyp Market (Amsterdam) - A Gastronomic Wonderland

Jump into the energetic scene of Albert Cuyp Market in Amsterdam. From neighborhood produce to global indulgences, this market is a blowout for the faculties. Investigate the slows down, for example, assorted flavors, and embrace the exuberant climate that characterizes Dutch road food culture.

As your culinary excursion through the Netherlands finishes up, may your recollections be loaded up with the wonderful preferences and smells that make Dutch cooking an exceptional encounter. Bon appétit!

6. SHOPPING IN UTRECHT

Welcome to the energetic shopping scene in Utrecht! As your educated local escort, I'll take you on a brilliant excursion through the city's exceptional gifts and various shopping regions.

Interesting Keepsakes: Reveal Fortunes from Utrecht

In Utrecht, gift shopping is an undertaking in itself. The city offers a variety of interesting remembrances that catch its rich history and contemporary appeal. For a particular keepsake, consider investigating the customary Dutch business sectors that dab the city. The blossom market hung on Oudegracht, is a visual dining experience with its kaleidoscope of varieties and scents. Here, you can get tulip bulbs or a bouquet to bring a hint of Dutch magnificence back home.

For those with an inclination for history, the Exhibition Hall Quarter is a mother lode of social trinkets. From reproductions of archaic relics to flawlessly created Delftware, you'll track down pieces that tell the story of Utrecht's past. Remember to investigate the beguiling autonomous shops along the channels, where nearby craft mans feature their abilities in high-quality adornments, earthenware production, and materials.

Shopping Regions: A Retail Sanctuary for Each Taste

Utrecht brags a varied blend of shopping areas, each with its particular person. How about we start our investigation in the core of the city:

Walking Around Oudegracht: The beat of Utrecht's shopping scene, Oudegracht is a beautiful waterway fixed with a variety of shops. From very good quality shops to peculiar one-of-a-kind stores, this clamoring region takes special care of every customer's taste. Take as much time as necessary as you explore the cobblestone roads, finding unexpected, yet invaluable treasures and beguiling bistros en route.

Hoog Catharijne: A Cutting Edge Shopping Haven: On the off chance that you favor a more contemporary shopping experience, go to Hoog Catharijne. This huge shopping center neighboring Utrecht Focal Station is a one-stop objective for style, hardware, and worldwide brands. Its cutting-edge design and various retail choices make it a helpful and dynamic shopping center.

Twijnstraat: An Enchanting Mix of Old and New: For a sample of Utrecht's verifiable appeal, Twijnstraat is a must-visit. This beguiling road, one of the most established in the city, is fixed with niche stores offering special items. Investigate the shops, enjoy distinctive chocolates, and relish the climate of this superb region.

Steekstraat and Zadelstraat: Stowed away Treasures: Adventure outside of what might be expected of Steekstraat and Zadelstraat, where secret fortunes are anticipated. These restricted roads are home to autonomous stores, exhibiting all that from design to home stylistic layout. It's the ideal spot to find something particular while submerging yourself in the neighborhood climate.

Utrechtse Market: A Worldwide Shopping Experience: On the off chance that you desire a multicultural shopping experience, Utrechtse Market is the spot to be. This vivacious market, held at Jaarbeurs, united merchants offering items from around the world. From flavors to materials, submerge yourself in the lively varieties and kinds of a worldwide commercial center.

Conclusion

As we finish up our shopping visit through Utrecht, we recollect that each region recounts a remarkable story, and each buy is a piece of that account. Whether you're chasing after immortal keepsakes or investigating present-day shopping shelters, Utrecht welcomes you to enjoy a retail experience like no other. Cheerful shopping!

7. NIGHTLIFE

Welcome to Utrecht, where the day's appeal consistently changes into dynamic evenings and outside undertakings. I'm your manual for the city's intriguing contributions, so how about we plunge into the subtleties?

Bars and Restaurants

In Utrecht, the night starts with a variety of bars and clubs along the notorious Oudegracht. Picture this: comfortable wharf basements transformed into barometrical bars. One champion is Bistro Olivier, a previous church offering a heavenly choice of nearby brews. Prepare to loosen up, talk with amicable local people, and assimilate the city's rich history in each taste.

Clubs and Entertainment

At the point when the night calls for more zing, Utrecht replies with its enthusiastic club scene. TivoliVredenburg, a multi-room scene, turns into a throbbing center point including different music occasions. Whether you're into electronic beats or live exhibitions, this is the spot to move your night away and absorb the electric climate.

Outdoor Activities

1. Parks and Gardens

Get away from the hustle in Utrecht's green sanctuaries. Griftpark, a neighborhood number one, welcomes you to loosen up by the lakes, investigate jungle gyms, and even offer a second with fuzzy companions at the petting zoo. Looking for a mix of nature and history? Utrecht College's professional flowerbeds are an herbal joy, offering a quiet retreat in the core of the city.

2. Cycling in Utrecht

Prepare to pedal your direction through the city's captivating excellence. Utrecht's level scene and cyclist-accommodating framework make it a heaven for bicycle devotees. Lease a bicycle and journey along beautiful waterways or adventure into the open country. It's not only a transportation method - it's an encounter, an opportunity to feel the city's pulse on two wheels.

3. Sporting Activities

For those anxious to blend relaxation in with experience, Utrecht conveys with different sporting exercises. Skim through the city's streams on a boat visit, paddle along the waterways, or embrace the excitement of kayaking. If just a little investigation, the Utrechtse Heuvelrug, a public park close by, anticipates climbing trails and stunning scenes.

From tasting creative mixes in noteworthy basements to cycling along pleasant waterways, Utrecht's nightlife and outside exercises offer an orchestra of encounters. Thus, gear up for an excursion loaded up with metropolitan fervor, normal excellence, and the warm hug of this Dutch diamond. Your Utrecht experience is standing by!

8. EVENTS AND FESTIVALS

Welcome, dear pilgrims, to a lively embroidery of occasions and celebrations that variety the schedule of our enchanting district. In this directed visit, we'll divulge the Yearly Occasions Schedule and investigate the Nearby Celebrations that make our local area beat with life.

1. Yearly Occasions Calendar

Our schedule unfurls like a very much prearranged play, every month offering a novel demonstration in the stupendous exhibition of local area festivity. In January, the town wakes up with the New Year's Function, where firecrackers paint the sky and chuckling resounds through the fresh air. It's a euphoric launch to the year, uniting families and companions.

As the days warm up, February proclaims the Adoration and Fellowship Celebration, a beguiling occasion where the roads are embellished with heart-formed enhancements. Whether you're walking inseparably with a friend or family member or savoring the delight of non-romantic associations, this celebration is a brilliant tribute to friendship.

Spring blasts forward with the Bloom March in Walk, a stunning showcase of botanical floats, dynamic outfits, and the sweet scent of sprouting blossoms. A scene catches the embodiment of recharging and nature's shine.

As the sun moves higher, April has the Spring Fair, a cornucopia of neighborhood makes, luscious treats, and vivacious music. The town square changes into a clamoring commercial center, reverberating with the chat of craft mans and the fragrance of luscious road food.

May takes us to the Social Combination Celebration, a festival of variety that grandstands the rich embroidery of customs woven into our local area. It's a dining experience for the faculties, with vivid exhibitions, enticing cooking styles, and a climate that spans the holes between societies.

June invites the Late spring Solstice Festivity, a cheerful social event on the longest day of the year. Huge fires, music, and a feeling of kinship light up the evening, making recollections that wait like the glow of a mid-year evening.

The musicality of life beats solid in July with the Town Festival, a kaleidoscope of carousels, and cotton treats slows down, and the euphoric giggling of youngsters. It's a nostalgic gesture to the straightforward delights of life, drawing families from all over.

August welcomes you to the Collect Celebration, where the air is imbued with the fragrance of ready products of the soil town square changes into a provincial shelter. It's a chance to respect the overflow of the time and offer appreciation for the bounties of nature.

September's feature is the Pre-Winter Equinox Ball, a refined undertaking that sees the local area wearing rich clothing for a night of dance and party. It's an enchanting mix of custom and class, catching the quintessence of the evolving seasons.

October embraces the creepy soul with the Halloween March, a scene of inventive ensembles and fun-loving dreads. Families and companions jump in and let loose, making it a memorable night.

November brings the Appreciation Assembling, an inspiring festival where the local area assembles to communicate much obliged. Shared feasts, stories, and the glow of shared appreciation make an environment of certifiable association.

The year finishes up with the Colder time of year Wonderland Celebration in December, a mystical scene of lights, snowflakes, and the jingle of ringers. A bubbly crescendo envelops the year with an embroidery of delight and miracle.

2. Nearby Festivals

Past the yearly schedule, our town is enhanced with embroidery of neighborhood celebrations that commend the extraordinary flavors and customs of our local area. The Mid-year Jazz Jam welcomes music fans to influence the deep tunes of neighborhood specialists, making a personal association among entertainers and the crowd.

The craft man Market, held every other month, changes the town square into a center point of innovativeness, with nearby specialists showing their products. It's a mother lode of high-quality merchandise, from unpredictably created gems to customized furniture, each piece recounting an account of expertise and energy.

Foodies celebrate during the Connoisseur Function, a celebration that exhibits the culinary gifts of our nearby gourmet experts. From connoisseur indulgences to road food places, a dining experience tempts taste buds and encourages a feeling of the local area through shared dinners.

The Eco-Fair is a demonstration of our obligation to supportability. Neighborhood natural drives, eco-accommodating items, and instructive studios join to motivate a greener approach to everyday life.

The Book Darlings' Mother Lode, held quarterly, coaxes book nuts to jump into a universe of scholarly enjoyments. Nearby writers, book clubs, and a comfortable perusing corner make it a safe house for the people who track down comfort in the composed word.

9. PRACTICAL INFORMATION

Welcome, individual pioneers, to Utrecht! We should jump into the bare essential subtleties that will make your excursion through this superb city smooth and vital.

Nearby Behavior

1. Good tidings and Gestures:

While meeting local people, a cordial gesture or handshake makes all the difference. Prepare yourself for the three-cheek kiss, a standard Dutch hello. Go ahead and respond or adhere to an old-fashioned handshake - one way or the other, you'll be heartily invited.

2. Shoes Off, Please:

Entering somebody's home or a customary Dutch spot? Remove those shoes! It's an honorable gesture and keeps the insides immaculate. Whenever welcome to a nearby home, a little gift or roses show appreciation for their friendliness.

3. Simple on the Volume:

In broad daylight spaces, keep discussions at a moderate volume. Utrecht people value a quiet and serene environment. Reliability is vital, so on the off chance that you're behind schedule, a well-mannered expression of remorse goes far.

4. Calm on Sundays:

On Sundays, the Dutch esteem their tranquility and calm. Many shops close early, and commotion levels drop.

Embrace the peaceful air and partake in a comfortable walk around the city.

5. Gain proficiency with a Little Dutch:

While numerous local people communicate in English, learning a couple of Dutch expressions adds an individual touch to your excursion. "Damp je wel" (thank you) and "Alsjeblieft" (please) are little motions that go quite far.

Utrecht Emergency Contacts

1. Dial 112 for Emergencies:

Need dire assistance? Dial 112 for police, fire, or health-related crises. The administrators communicate in English, guaranteeing you get the help you want immediately.

2. Non-Crisis Police Matters:

For less dire police concerns, dial 0900-8844. They're there to assist with lost property, minor occurrences, or whatever doesn't need quick consideration.

3. Medical care Assistance:

If there should be an occurrence of medical problems, go to the UMC Utrecht emergency clinic. The crisis office can be reached at +31 88 755 5555. It's wise to have travel protection covering clinical costs for the inward feeling of harmony.

4. Government office Contacts:

Know the area and contact subtleties of your consulate. They can help with identification issues, crises, or any unforeseen circumstances you might experience.

5. Nearby Pharmacies:

For minor illnesses or normal prescriptions, drug stores (apotheeks) are boundless. Search for the green cross sign, and you'll find a cordial drug specialist prepared to help.

Valuable Tips for Explorers

1. Embrace Biking:

Utrecht is a safe house that welcomes bicycles. Lease a bicycle to investigate the city nearby. With all around kept up with bicycle paths, you'll float through the enchanting trenches and noteworthy roads.

2. Public Vehicle Savvy:

The OV-chipkaart is your pass to a public vehicle. Get it at train stations or grocery stores for issue-free transport and train rides. Taxis are accessible yet can be pricier than public vehicle choices.

3. English is Your Friend:

English is generally spoken, making correspondence a breeze. In any case, sprinkle in a couple of Dutch expressions for that additional appeal. Local people will see the value in the work.

4. Culinary Adventures:

Utrecht flaunts a different culinary scene. Try not to miss stroopwafels, Dutch cheddar, and bitterballen. Investigate nearby business sectors like Vredenburg for new produce, blossoms, and interesting gifts.

5. Climate Misfortunes and Festivals:

Pack layers and consistently have an umbrella helpful - Utrecht's weather conditions can be unusual. Check the neighborhood occasions schedule for celebrations and festivities, adding a layer of satisfaction to your visit.

All in all outfitted with nearby decorum, crisis contacts, and these convenient tips, you're set for an astounding Utrecht experience. Absorb the magnificence, appreciate the flavors, and partake in each second in this Dutch jewel. Safe voyages!

10. DAY TRIPS FROM UTRECHT

Road Trips from Utrecht: Investigating Close by Urban Communities and Attractions

Welcome to Utrecht, a beguiling city with its novel person and an ideal center point for investigating the encompassing miracles. In this aide, we'll dig into the awesome road trips you can set out on from Utrecht, finding close by urban communities and attractions that guarantee to advance your movement experience.

Close-by Urban communities and Attractions

I. Amsterdam: The Capital Extravaganza

Simply a short train ride away, Amsterdam coaxes with its notable waterways, memorable design, and lively culture. Investigate the Van Gogh Gallery, walk around the beautiful Jordaan region, or take a relaxed waterway journey. Amsterdam's appeal is certain to enthrall you.

II. Rotterdam: Current Marvels

Jump on a train to Rotterdam, a city that easily mixes innovation with custom. Wonder about the trying engineering, including the Shape Houses and Erasmus Extension. Try not to miss the Markthal, a foodie sanctuary where you can enjoy different culinary joys.

III. The Hague: Imperial Resonance

Find the political heart of the Netherlands in The Hague. Visit the Binnenhof, where the Dutch government dwells, and investigate the Mauritshuis to respect magnum opuses like Vermeer's "Young Lady with a Pearl Stud." The Hague's magnificent feeling is a treat for history fans.

IV. Giethoorn: Venice of the North

For a quiet departure, go to Giethoorn, frequently named the "Venice of the North." Explore through its enchanting trenches by boat and respect the covered rooftop cabins. Giethoorn offers a tranquil retreat, an unmistakable difference to the clamoring energy of Utrecht.

V. Keukenhof Nurseries: Sprouts in Abundance

Springtime uncovers a flower heaven at Keukenhof Nurseries. A short drive from Utrecht, this charming objective features a huge number of tulips and other dynamic blossoms. Go for a comfortable walk through fastidiously finished gardens for an explosion of variety and scent.

Transportation for Day Trips

I. Trains: Proficient and Scenic

Utrecht's focal area makes it a center point for an effective and beautiful training organization. Dutch Railroads (NS) associates Utrecht with significant urban areas, permitting you to cross the nation serenely. Appreciate beautiful perspectives on the way to Amsterdam, Rotterdam, and then some.

II. Bikes: Dutch Delight

Embrace the neighborhood way of life by cycling to local objections. Utrecht is famous for its bicycle accommodating framework, and leasing a bike is a magnificent method for investigating the grand open country or adventure into adjoining urban communities. Pedal your approach to unlikely treasures outside of what might be expected.

III. Vehicle Rentals: Opportunity to Roam

For those looking for adaptability, vehicle rentals allow you to investigate at your speed. Reveal enchanting towns, visit palaces settled in the open country, and make your customized schedule. Remember that stopping in downtown areas might require some preparation.

IV. Directed Visits: Peaceful Exploration

Pick directed visits if you lean toward a problem-free encounter. Various visit administrators offer journeys from Utrecht to different objections, giving shrewd discourse and dealing with coordinated factors.

11. CONCLUSION

Final Thoughts and Recommendations

As our visit through this tremendous scene of data concludes, how about we stop and ponder the key sights we've investigated? In this last section, we'll dig into a few definitive considerations and give proposals for your proceeding with the venture.

Last Considerations

Our investigation started with the basic scene of information, where we explored the valleys of key ideas. From language subtleties to verifiable milestones, we've covered a different landscape. It's urgent to see the value in the interconnectedness of these thoughts, similar to the multifaceted trap of a bug, where each string adds to the strength of the entirety.

In navigating the scholarly scenes, it's apparent that the landscape is consistently developing. New pinnacles arise, and old valleys extend with time. The end, in this way, isn't an endpoint but an achievement in a continuous excursion. Keep in mind that the quest for information isn't a run; it's a long-distance race where each step is a step toward understanding.

Suggestions

As you proceed with your endeavor, think about these proposals as your directing compass:

I. Hug Interest

In the domain of information, interest is the compass that guides you to unfamiliar regions. Make sure to ask questions, challenge suspicions, and investigate the unexplored world. It's through interest that we uncover unexpected, yet invaluable treasures and make significant associations between apparently dissimilar ideas.

II. Enhance Your Way

Similarly, as a balanced visit takes you through different attractions, a comprehensive way to deal with learning includes investigating different subjects. Adventure past your usual range of familiarity, and you'll find surprising associations that enhance your comprehension. Keep in mind that the most amazing perspectives frequently lie off in an unexpected direction.

III. Interface with Individual Voyagers

Information is certainly not a single pursuit. Draw in with a local area of individual students, share bits of knowledge, and participate in significant conversations. The trading of thoughts encourages a cooperative air where everybody benefits from the aggregate insight of the gathering.

IV. Consider the Excursion

Take minutes to stop, think back, and value how far you've come. Consider the bits of knowledge acquired, the difficulties surviving, and the development accomplished. It's in these intelligent stops that the meaning of the excursion turns out to be clear, and the subsequent stages come into the center.

V. Hug Deep-rooted Learning

The finish of this visit doesn't check the finish of your learning process. Embrace the way of thinking of long-lasting learning. Similarly, as a city consistently develops, so does the scene of information. Remain open to groundbreaking thoughts, adjust to change, and let your journey for figuring out be a long-lasting experience.

Last Objective

All in all, the territory we've covered together is only a preview of the immense scholarly scene anticipating investigation. As you leave on your singular process, recall that this isn't a goodbye but a bon journey. The excellence of information lies in its obtaining as well as in the consistent investigation and use of what you've realized.

Thus, individual adventurers, convey these last considerations and proposals with you as you explore the scenes of understanding. The excursion is yours to shape, and the disclosures are holding back to unfurl with each step you take.

Printed in Great Britain
by Amazon

63055098R00057